First World War
and Army of Occupation
War Diary
France, Belgium and Germany

41 DIVISION
122 Infantry Brigade
East Surrey Regiment
9th and 12th Battalion
1 April 1919 - 31 October 1919

WO95/2634/1

The Naval & Military Press Ltd
www.nmarchive.com
Published in association with The National Archives

Published by

The Naval & Military Press Ltd

Unit 10 Ridgewood Industrial Park,

Uckfield, East Sussex,

TN22 5QE England

Tel: +44 (0) 1825 749494

www.naval-military-press.com

www.nmarchive.com

This diary has been reprinted in facsimile from the original. Any imperfections are inevitably reproduced and the quality may fall short of modern type and cartographic standards.

© **Crown Copyright**
Images reproduced by permission of The National Archives, London, England, 2015.

Contents

Document type	Place/Title	Date From	Date To
Heading	WO95/2634/1		
Heading	9th Bn East Surrey Regt Apr-Oct 1919		
War Diary	Marialinden	01/04/1919	11/04/1919
War Diary	Volberg	12/04/1919	30/04/1919
Operation(al) Order(s)	122nd Infantry Brigade Operation Order No. 264	06/04/1919	06/04/1919
Miscellaneous	Defence Scheme		
Miscellaneous	Headquarters, London Division, "G"	09/04/1919	09/04/1919
Miscellaneous	Section VI Disposition Of Troops and Action in case of attack.	10/04/1919	10/04/1919
Miscellaneous	Appendix "A"		
Miscellaneous	March Table "A". "Move to positions of Readiness."		
War Diary	March Table "B". "Move to Battle positions."		
Miscellaneous	March Table C. "Occupy Much-Drabenderhoe Line."		
Miscellaneous	Appendix "B"		
Miscellaneous	Appendix "C"		
Miscellaneous	Appendix "D"		
War Diary	Volberg	01/05/1919	12/05/1919
War Diary	Volberg Kalk	14/05/1919	14/05/1919
War Diary	Kalk	15/05/1919	30/06/1919
Miscellaneous	Nominal Roll Of Officers	26/06/1919	26/06/1919
Miscellaneous	Nominal Roll Of Officers	30/07/1919	30/07/1919
Miscellaneous	H. Q., 1st London Brigade.	01/08/1919	01/08/1919
War Diary	Koln Kalk	01/07/1919	09/07/1919
War Diary	Kalk	10/07/1919	15/07/1919
War Diary	Ehreshoven	16/07/1919	01/09/1919
War Diary	Eugelslcircheu	02/09/1919	31/10/1919
Miscellaneous	Nominal Roll Of Officers.	01/10/1919	01/10/1919
War Diary	Nominal Roll Of Officers.		

work / 3634 (1)

work / 3634 (1)

LONDON DIVISION
(LATE 41ST DIVISION)
122ND INFY BDE

9TH BN EAST SURREY REGT

APR - OCT 1919

FROM 24 DIV
72 BDE

Army Form C. 2118.

A. of O.

WAR DIARY
or
INTELLIGENCE SUMMARY.
(Erase heading not required.)

9th BATTALION,
EAST SURREY
REGIMENT.

No. ....
Date ..6/4/19..............

Instructions regarding War Diaries and Intelligence Summaries are contained in F. S. Regs., Part II. and the Staff Manual respectively. Title pages will be prepared in manuscript.

Place	Date	Hour	Summary of Events and Information	Remarks and references to Appendices
MARIALINDEN	1/4/19		Leave is still going well and the men are delighted.	
do	2/4/19		The Divisional Commander visits the two new coys. at training and the H.Q. coy. He is well satisfied with the inspection.	
do	3/4/19		Carry on training with our Lewis Gunners and signallers and any men we have left. Still sending men down to work on the new Rifle Range at OVERATH.	
do	4/4/19		The Divisional Commander visits the outpost line will our R.S.C. Brigadier General Ramsay C.M.G. D.S.O. He again expresses himself pleased with the way things are carried out.	
do	5/4/19		Training continues in the morning. We play the 17nd Middlesex at football and win 2 goals to Nil.	
do	6/4/19		The church parade to day as we have an inter company relief on. "A" Coy relieves "B" Coy on the left subsector. "D" Coy relieves "C" Coy on the Right subsector.	

WAR DIARY
or
INTELLIGENCE SUMMARY

Army Form C. 2118.

Place	Date	Hour	Summary of Events and Information	Remarks and references to Appendices
Narratunderra	6/4/19	Cont	In accordance with Brigade instructions a practice with drawal takes place and our two supporting companies move up as reinforcements.	
do.	7/4/19		Carry on with our working parties and training – nothing of interest to report.	
do.	8/4/19		Picquets for the B.G.C. inspection of Transport. "O" Coy busily felling young fir trees for the Divisional Horse jumping competition.	
do.	9/4/19		Lt. Col. Heath CMG DSO Commanding the 23rd Middlesex Regt. comes up to arrange details of relief. The 23rd Middlesex Regt. will relieve us in the outpost line on the 12th inst.	
do.	10/4/19		B.G.C. inspects the transport and is quite satisfied with the turn out though we only have men men and half our own horses.	[signature]

Army Form C. 2118.

WAR DIARY
or
INTELLIGENCE SUMMARY.
(Erase heading not required.)

Instructions regarding War Diaries and Intelligence Summaries are contained in F. S. Regs., Part II. and the Staff Manual respectively. Title pages will be prepared in manuscript.

Place	Date	Hour	Summary of Events and Information	Remarks and references to Appendices
MARIALINDEN	11/4/19		Advance party of 23rd Middlesex arrive to take over billets and see posts. The C.O. Adjutant Transport Officer and Sgt. Fry leaves for the Divisional Race Meeting.	
VOLBERG	12/4/19		Battalion moves to the VOLBERG area in Brigade Transport Reserve. It rains heavily the whole time and the men are soaked through.	
"	13/4/19		Sunday. Church parade.	
"	14/4/19		Start training and education according to programme. We still have very few men owing to leave.	
"	15/4/19		The Divisional Commander and B.G.C. inspect the Transport and express satisfaction on the turn out.	
"	16/4/19		Training continues	
"	17/4/19		Education scheme in full swing all the men are being classified.	
"	18/4/19		Good Friday. Church parade in the morning and football matches in afternoon	
"	19/4/19		Everyone out cutting brushwood for Divisional Race Meeting	[signature]

Army Form C. 2118.

WAR DIARY
or
INTELLIGENCE SUMMARY.
(Erase heading not required.)

Instructions regarding War Diaries and Intelligence Summaries are contained in F.S. Regs., Part II. and the Staff Manual respectively. Title pages will be prepared in manuscript.

Place	Date	Hour	Summary of Events and Information	Remarks and references to Appendices
VOLBERG.	20/4/19		Easter Sunday. Church Parade and Special Service	
do	21/4/19		A general holiday. Sports and games	
do	22/4/19		Training continues. B.G.C. inspects Unit Regtl. Cards and Orderly Room and is well satisfied.	
do	23/4/19		Nothing special to report.	
do	24/4/19		Education and training continues	
do	25/4/19		Ditto - nothing of interest to report.	
do	26/4/19		The Divisional Commander inspects the companies at training. A guard is detailed for Bde H.Q. and is inspected by the Brigade and Divisional Commanders who express their satisfaction.	
do	27/4/19		Church Parade	
do	28/4/19		First day of the London Divisional Race Meeting. We have one entry for the Fire Furlong flat race - Ralph Seurry. The mare "Buffles" gets 21/4/11	

WAR DIARY
or
INTELLIGENCE SUMMARY.
(Erase heading not required.)

Army Form C. 2118.

Place	Date	Hour	Summary of Events and Information	Remarks and references to Appendices
VOLBERG	and		Moved as third. Lieut Col. S.A. Connor's "Gallant" and "Somme" are entered for the Cologne Chase.	
do	29/4/19		Second Day of the Races. The Battalion sends about 200 men each day as spectators. The meeting is a great success and very well attended. Training continues.	JMBM
do	30/4/19			

Runcolnur
Lieut Col. Comdg.
9th Batt Surrey Regt.

SECRET.   Copy No.....2......

122ND INFANTRY BRIGADE OPERATION ORDER NO.264.

Reference maps - Sheets 2910 and 2911 - 1/25,000.

1. 23rd Middlesex Regt. will relieve the 9th East Surrey Regt. in the Outpost Line on Saturday 12th instant.

2. The 9th East Surrey Regt. will, on relief, move to VOLBERG Area, into Brigade Reserve.

3. All arrangements for relief to be made by Battalion Commanders concerned.

4. Command of the Outpost Line will pass to Lt.Col.HEATH, C.M.G., D.S.O., on completion of relief.

5. Completion of relief to be reported to this office.

6. 20 Lorries will report to H.Q. 23rd. Middlesex Regt., HOFFNUNGSTHAL, at 07.30 hours on April 12th., 14 for conveying the 8 Platoons due to relieve the picquets on the perimeter of the Bridgehead, and 6 for packs, blankets etc.
   The same lorries will be available for the 9th East Surrey Regt. on the return journey.

7. Demonstration Platoon detailed for the Brigade School will now be found by the 9th East Surrey Regt., and will be accommodated with the Battalion in HOFFNUNGSTHAL.

8. Units of Brigade Group to Acknowledge.

S.R. Hoff

Captain,
Brigade Major,
122nd. Infantry Brigade.

Issued at 22.00 hours
6.4.19.

-0-0-0-0-0-0-0-0-

1. File.
2. War Diary.
3. London Division.
4.   -do-
5. 9th East Surrey Regt.
6. 7th Middlesex Regt.
7. 23rd Middlesex Regt.
8. C.R.A., London Division.
9. A.D.M.S.   -do-
10. D.A.P.M.   -do-
11. 138th Field Ambulance.
12. 228th Field Company, R.E.
13. B. Company, M.G.Corps.
14. B. Battery, 190th Bde. R.F.A.
15. 190 Brigade, R.F.A.
16. 123rd Infantry Brigade.
17. 124th Infantry Brigade.
18. 103rd   -do-
19. No.2. Company, Div. Train.
20. Brigade Major.
21. Staff Captain.
22. Brigade Signal Officer.

-0-0-0-0-0-

SECRET.   *War Diary* Copy No..2......

DEFENCE SCHEME.

Right Sub-Sector.   Right Division.   VI Corps.

Reference maps:- Sheet 2910 - 1/25,000 - OVERATH.
                    "   2011 -   "   - ENGELSKIRCHEN.

CONTENTS.

1. Brigade Sector.
2. Boundaries.
3. Description of the Country.
4. Defensive system.
5. Policy of Occupation.
6. Disposition of Troops and action in case of attack.
7. Vickers Guns.
8. Points of Observation.
9. Defensive Organisation of Artillery.

APPENDICES.

"A" Concentration March Tables.
"B" Standing Orders for Sentry Posts.
"C" Detailed dispositions of troops in Outpost Line.
"D" Signal Communications.
"E" Detail of Bridge over River AGGER.

MAPS.

"A" Boundaries, Defensive Line, Machine Gun Positions.

-o-o-o-o-o-o-o-o-

DISTRIBUTION.

1. File.
2. War Diary.
3. 9th East Surrey Regt.
4. 7th Middlesex Regt.
5. 23rd Middlesex Regt.
6. 190th Brigade, R.F.A.
7. B. Battery, 190th Bde R.F.A.
8. 228th Field Company, R.E.
9. 158th Field Ambulance.
10. "B" Coy. 41st. M.G.Corps.
11. No.2.Company, Divl. Train.
12. London Division "G".
13. London Division "Q".
14. C.R.A., London Division.
15. C.R.E., London Division.
16. A.D.M.S., London Division.
17. D.A.P.M., London Division.
18. 2nd London Infantry Brigade.
19. 3rd London Infantry Brigade.
20. 103rd Infantry Brigade.
21. Staff Captain Civil Duties.
22. D.A.P.M., ROSRATH.
23. G.O.C., Brigade.
24. Brigade Major.
25. Staff Captain.
26. Brigade Signal Officer.
27 - 46. 1st London Inf.Bde. School.
47. Spare.
48. Spare.
49. Spare.
50. Spare.

1. Brigade Sector.

The 1st London Brigade, London Division, holds the Right Sub-Sector of the front of the Right Division, VI Corps. (Cologne Bridgehead).

The Eastern Division is on the Right, junction at F 9,3 - 6,6.

The 3rd London Brigade, London Division, is on the Left, junction at S 8,7 - 4,9.

2. Boundaries.

The Military Northern and Southern Boundaries are shown on Map "A".

The Boundaries for Civil Administration do not necessarily coincide with the Military Boundaries; the Civil Boundaries are drawn to coincide as far as possible with the present German Boundaries of each respective Burgermeisterei.

The radius of the Bridgehead is twenty miles; the Eastern Boundary has been adjusted to conform with the Communal Civil Boundaries and runs :-

From junction with Southern Division at the bend of the NAAF, three quarters of a mile N.E. of HOLL - along the NAAF B. to ABELSNAAF - HECK - along road to DRABENDERHOHE (exclusive) - N. along road through BRUCHEN, thence along stream to HALTENBACH (exclusive) to HARDT (inclusive)

3. Description of the Country.

From the valley of the Rhine Eastwards, the ground gradually rises in gentle slopes as far as the river SULZ. East of the River SULZ the country becomes very hilly and broken, being inter-sected with deep valleys, and ravines with steep convex slopes. The ravines are wooded affording good cover, and there are numerous copses on the hillsides.

From the River RHINE to a general line drawn North to South about one mile East of the main HEUMAR - WAHN Road, the country is open, and, being thickly populated, is covered with innumerable small houses and factories.

Further East, as far as the R. SULZ, the area is entirely forest called KONIGSFORST, through which are cut numerous straight "Rides" and tracks.

The area topographically divides itself into three zones, these divisions being made by the AGGER and SULZ Rivers, both running approx. North and South across the area. These are both fordable, except after heavy rains.

The roads along the valleys of the river AGGER and SULZ, together with the MARIALINDEN - MUCH Road, form the main arteries of traffic.

There are three lines of Railways :-
1. Running from COLOGNE to SIEBURG, then up the valley of the AGGER through OVERATH to ENGELSKIRCHEN, and thence on to the neutral zone.
2. Running from COLOGNE via ROSRATH to LINDLAR up the valley of the SULZ. A lateral connects the line from HOFFNUNGSTHAL to OVERATH.
3. Running from COLOGNE via BERG GLADBACH to ROSRATH where it joins No.2.

The main tactical features within the area forward of the river AGGER are :-

      (a) Hill 229.   BUSCHOVEN.
      (b) Hill 247.   East of WARTH
      (c) MARIALINDEN.
      (d) Hill 324.   East of MUCH
      (e) Hill 309.   South of HUNDEHAUSEN.

4. Defensive System. Map "A".

At present no trenches exist.

The primary object of the Bridgehead Position is to secure the passages of the RHINE so as to enable a force being concentrated East of the Rhine without interference by the enemy.

With this object in view, work on defences has been commenced in the following order :-
- (a) Wire.
- (b) Spitlocking of trenches.
- (c) Digging, draining and revetting.

The construction of concrete pill-boxes is being carried out simultaneously with the other work.

It is not intended that wiring will be continuous throughout the whole length of the line.

All approaches and the ground swept by machine guns will, however, be wired in such a manner as to detain the attackers under fire.

The Brigade Area is organised on the following lines :-
(a) i. The Outpost Line, which consists of a series of eight posts along the outer perimeter, commanding all roads, approaches, and exits to and from the neutral zone.
  ii. The Outpost Line of Resistance, consisting of a series of strong points and Defended Localities.
(b) The Main Line of Resistance, which is the front line of the Battle Zone, consisting of a series of defended localities and Strong Points along the main tactical features described in para 3. Each locality will be strongly wired and be capable of all round defence.

The Main Line of Resistance within the Divisional Boundaries, is divided into three Brigade sub-sections.
(c) The Support Line of the Main Line of Resistance, which is situated on the West Bank of the River AGGER,/HONRATH - to hold the crossings of the River at

The Infantry will be supported by Field Artillery and Machine Guns as follows :-
(a) By Field Guns, so sighted to support the Defence of the Main Line of Resistance, and by the Field Guns of forward batteries supporting the outposts. The guns will not be actually placed in position, but positions and O.Ps. will be selected and marked.
(b) By Machine Guns placed in Defended Localities, and in position to cover the ground between Strong Points.

The Machine Guns will not actually be placed in position, but positions will be sighted and prepared.

----

5. Policy of Occupation.

The tactical organisation of the area is drawn up with a view to offensive rather than defensive action; and preparations are made to permit of the rapid concentration of the Division prior to a further advance Eastward.

Principle of Defence.

When completed the sector will be held in depth, the Outpost Line as lightly as possible.

In each Company there will always be one platoon, and in each Battalion one company, available for counter-attacks.

There will be no withdrawal from the Main Line of Resistance.

In the event of a general attack along the line, the troops occupying the Front System, that is, the ground forward of the Main Line of Resistance defined in para. 4, will not be reinforced from or behind the above mentioned line.

The role of the troops in advance of the Main Line of Resistance is to give warning of an enemy attack, to repulse it if possible, or failing that, to delay the enemy advance for sufficient length of time to enable the Support Battalion to move up and occupy the Main Line of Resistance.

If ultimately forced by superior numbers to evacuate the Outpost Zone, they will withdraw fighting behind the Main Line of Resistance and reform behind MARIALINDEN.

In addition, the Right Company of the Outpost Battalion, finding Examining Posts Nos. 1 to 4 inclusive, will be prepared on receipt of orders to move forward in an easterly direction, and establish Outposts on the General Line LUCH (exclusive) to DRADENDERHOHE, occupying the high ground Hill 324 (Square X 96) and Hill 309 (Square Y 0.8), keeping in touch during such forward movement with the Outpost of the Right Division, who will be advancing at the same time to the line HULSCHERD - MUCH (inclusive).

Headquarters,
   London Division, "G".

Forwarded.

9/4/19.
                        Brigadier General,
              Commanding 122nd. Infantry Brigade.

SECTION VI.
Disposition of Troops and Action in case of attack.

1. "A" Battalion in the Outpost System, disposed as follows:-

   Two Companies holding the examining posts in the outer perimeter i.e. each post held by one platoon.
   Two Companies in Support in MARIALINDEN.
   Battalion Headquarters are at MARIALINDEN.
   In the event of a hostile attempt to penetrate the Outpost Line, the forward posts will offer the greatest resistance and delay the enemy as long as possible; if forced to retire, they will do so rear-fighting, to successive positions, to the Outpost Line of Resistance, which they will occupy in conjunction with the remaining 2 companies moving from MARIALINDEN. (Vide following para.)
   The two companies accommodated in MARIALINDEN will move to and occupy the Outpost Line of Resistance. (Each company keeping one platoon in reserve.)
   It is imperative that the Outpost Line of Resistance be held for at least four hours to enable the Support Battalion to move up and occupy the Main Line of Resistance.

   Battalion Battle Headquarters will be established at LA'DUEHR.

   There will be no withdrawal from the Outpost Line of Resistance without orders from Brigade Headquarters.
   If the order for withdrawal is given, the Outpost Battalion will retire behind MARIALINDEN, re____ and will come into Brigade Reserve.

2. "B" Battalion in Support, accommodated as follows:-

   Two Companies in OVERATH.
   One Company in HAUS AUEL. (Sq.W 6,5)
   One Company in STEINENBRUCK.
   Battalion Headquarters are at OVERATH.
   The role of the Battalion in Support is to move up and occupy the Main Line of Resistance, with three companies in the line, and one company in Battalion Reserve behind hill 247, (East of WARTH).
   Battalion Battle Headquarters will be at MARIALINDEN.
   The Battalion in Support will not be used for counter attacks in front of the Main Line of Resistance, except to re-establish the front system in case of penetration in a purely local attack.

3. "C" Battalion in Brigade Reserve accommodated as follows:-

   Two Companies in HOFFNUNGSTHAL.
   One Company in UNTER and OBER LUGHAUSEN (East of HOFFNUNGSTHAL).
   One company (Detached) at HOHKEPPEL.
   Battalion Headquarters are at HOFFNUNGSTHAL.
   The role of "C" Battalion (less detached company) in reserve is to move to HONRATH and be prepared to:-
   (a) Reinforce the Main Line of Resistance between the Brigade Boundaries.
   (b) Carry out Counter attacks upon
       BUSCHHOVEN.
       Hill 247, (East of WARTH)
       MARIALINDEN.
   (c) Take up a defensive position on the high ground East of HONRATH in square W 6,6 to co____ the crossings of the River AGGER.
   The role of the detached company is to move forward and occupy the Main Line of Resistance from TREPEN (inclusive) through ALEMICH to the Brigade Northern Boundary (i.e. the "Occupation" boundary) on the East bank of the River AGGER.
   The valley of the AGGER is inclusive to the Brigade on the left, who are responsible for its defence.
   The detached company will hold the Main Line of Resistance defined above until relieved by the Centre Brigade coming from Division Reserve upon which they will concentrate on Brucke, East of OVERATH.

4. The following orders will be sent from Brigade Headquarters :-

(a) Move to Position of Readiness.
   (b) Man Battle Positions.
   (c) Occupy Much-Drabenderhohe Line.

5. **On receipt of (a).**
"A" and "B" Battalions will stand by, ready to resume the advance, or move to Battle Positions.

"C" Battalion, less detached company, will move at once to HONRATH.

"C" Battalion, detached company only, will stand by at HOHKEPPEL.

Batteries located in the forward area will occupy positions in support of the Outpost Battalion, and remaining batteries of affiliated Artillery Brigade will move forward, by previously reconnoitred routes, to previously selected assembly areas.

228th. Field Company R.E. will stand by at HONRATH.

"B" Coy., 41st. Bn. M.G.C. will move as follows:-
    1 Section to HONRATH.
    1½ Sections to MARIALINDEN to report to O/C. "A" Battalion for the defence of the Outpost Line of Resistance.
    1½ Sections to OVERATH.

The Reserve Brigade will be moved forward, under Divisional Orders, to an assembly area about ESCHBACH-IMMEKEPPEL.

6. **On receipt of (b).**
"A" Battalion will occupy Battle Positions.

"B" Battalion will move to and occupy the Main Line of Resistance between the Brigade Boundaries. The Northern Boundary for this operation will be a line drawn through points:- X 0,3-9,7. to S 2,9-0,7 (SIEFEN inclusive).

The Southern Boundary remains unchanged.

"C" Battalion, detached company only, will move to and occupy the Main Line of Resistance, from SIEFEN (inclusive) through ALEMICK to the Brigade Northern Boundary (i.e. the "Occupation" boundary) on the East Bank of the River AGGER, which line they will hold until relieved by the Centre Brigade.

On relief they will concentrate at BRUCHE, East of Karth OVERATH.

"C" Battalion, less detached company, will stand by at HONRATH, and will be responsible for holding the crossings of the River AGGER. (vide Section VI para 3 c supra)

Affiliated batteries of Divisional Artillery will move to and occupy positions already prepared to cover the Main Line of Resistance.

228th. Field Company R.E. will stand by at HONRATH.

"B" Coy. 41st. B. M.G.C. will move as follows:-
    1½ Sections for MARIALINDEN to the Outpost Line of Resistance.

    1½ Sections for OVERATH, and 1 Section for HONRATH will move to and occupy the Main Line of Resistance in conjunction with "B" Battalion.

1st. (London) Infantry Brigade Headquarters, will move to OVERATH.

The Reserve Brigade will move, under Divisional Orders, to occupy the Main Line of Resistance. (Centre Sub-Sector)

7. **On receipt of (c).**
"A" Battalion will swing forward their right and establish outposts on the general line MUCH (exclusive)-DRABENDERHOHE (inclusive) to present junction with the left Brigade at S 8,7-4,9, occupying the high ground Hill 324 (Sq.X96) and Hill 309 (Sq.Y.0.8).

During the forward movement close touch will be maintained with the troops of the right Division, which will be advancing at the same time to the line HULSCHEID-MUCH (inclusive).

Battalion Battle Headquarters plus 2 companies in Reserve will concentrate at No.6 Post. (heck b)

"B" Battalion will concentrate at FEDERATH.

"C" Battalion, less detached company, will concentrate at MARIALINDEN.

"C" Battalion, detached company only, will concentrate at UNTER-VILKERATH and await orders.

Batteries located in the forward area will take up positions to cover the MUCH-KALTENBACH Line, as defined above, the remaining batteries of the affiliated Artillery Brigade moving forward to MARIALINDEN.

228th. Field Coy.R.E. will concentrate at MARIALINDEN.
"B"Coy.41st.Bn.M.G.C. will detail 1½ Sections (six guns) to report to O/C "A" Battalion for the defence of the MUCH-KALTENBACH Line: the remaining 2½ Sections (10 guns) concentrating in FEDERATH.

    1st.(London) Infantry Brigade Headquarters will be established in FEDERATH.

7. Vickers Machine Guns.

One Company (16 guns) is affiliated to the Right Brigade, and is accommodated at BLEIFELD.
In the event of hostilities, the Company will be disposed as follows :-

1½ Sections (6 guns) covering the Outpost Line of Resistance.
2½ Sections (10 guns) covering the Main Line of Resistance.
Company Battle H.Q. will be established at MARIALINDEN.
Defensive Positions are shown on Map "A".

8. Points of Observation.

Points from which observation can be obtained are :-

Hill 247, East of WARTH.
MARIALINDEN.
The perimeter of the Outpost Line between DRABENDERHOHE and KOLTERBACH.

9. Defensive Organisation of Artillery.

The Sector is covered by the 190th Brigade, R.F.A., which is accommodated as follows :-
1 18 pdr. battery at OVERATH.
2 18 pdr. batteries at DEUTZ.
1 4.5" Howitzer Battery at DEUTZ.
Artillery Brigade Head quarters are at DEUTZ.

The role of the Forward battery is to maintain touch with, and be in immediate support of the Outpost Battalion by engaging routes and approaches etc.
On receipt of orders from G.O.C. Right Infantry Brigade, affiliated Artillery Brigade H.Q. plus two 18 pdr. batteries and one 4.5" Howitzer Battery, will move forward, concentrating in the first place on road W 4,9 - 9,0, STEIMENBRUCK, and from there moving forward and occupying positions in support of the Main Line of Resistance as the situation may require.
One 18 pdr. battery from the Right Brigade, and one 18 pdr. battery from the Left Brigade, will pass to the tactical control of the G.O.C. Centre Infantry Brigade as soon as he takes over responsibility for the defence of the centre sub-sector.
Two 18 pdr. batteries and one 4.5" Howitzer Battery will then remain at the disposal of the G.O.C. Right Infantry Brigade, for the Defence of the Right Sub-Sector.

10/4/19

APPENDIX "A".

March Tables A, B, and C.

Table A.   "Move to Positions of Readiness."

Table B.   "Move to Battle Positions."

Table C.   "Occupy MUCH - DRABENDERHOHE."

The tables have been worked out on the following basis :-

(a) That a previous warning had been received and units were standing to, ready to move at half an hours notice. 30 minutes must therefore be added to each time to include time taken to "turn out".
(b) That the average rate of marching would not exceed more than two miles per hour, in view of the steep and long hills and also the heavy surface of certain of the roads and tracks which will necessarily have to be followed.
(c) That in all marches exceeding four hours, an hours halt will be necessary. The extra hour has been allowed for in the table.

The march of the affiliated Field Ambulance is not included as it is not yet known which ambulance will be allotted to the Brigade.

MARCH TABLE "A". "Move to positions of Readiness."

Serial No.	Unit.	From	To.	Starting Point Position	Time.	Route.	In Final position by.	R'mks.
1.	"A"Battn.	—	—	—	—	—	—	Will not move
2.	"B"Battn.	—	—	—	—	—	—	-do-
3.	"C"Battn.(less detached Coy) 2 Companies.	Hoffnungsthal	Honrath.	Bridge over R.SULZ. VOIDE N. Coy.H.Q.	Z.	Level Crossing W3,2-7,5. Klein-Eigen-Linden.	Z + 2hrs.	
4.	"C"Battn.(detached Coy.only)	L Company LUGHAUSEN	-do-	Z.	Stocken-Linden.	Z + 2hrs.		
							Will not move.	
5.	"B"Batt.190Bde. (Advanced Batt)	Overath.	Marialinden.	Overath Ch.	Z.	Bridge W8,3-9,8	Z + 1hr.	
6.	228th.Field Coy.R.E.	—	—	—	—	—	—	Will not move.
7.	"B"Coy.M.G.C.(1½Sect)	Bleifeld	Marialinden	Fork Rds. W 4,8-8,0	Z	Heiligenhaus-Overath.	Z + 2hr.28mins.	
	(1 Sect.)	Bleifeld	Honrath	-do-	Z	Direct.	Z + 40mins.	
	(1½Sect)	Bleifeld	Overath		Z	Heiligenhaus-Overath.	Z + 1hr.28mins.	
8.	A.C.& D Batt.190Bde.	Deutz	Steinenbruck area	Under orders of O/C 190 Bde. R.F.A.	—	Bensberg-Unter Eschbach.	Z + 5hrs.	
9.	1st.London Inf.Bde.H.Q.	—	—	—	—	—	—	Will not move.

MARCH TABLE B. "Move to Battle Positions."

Serial No.	Unit	From.	To.	Starting point. Position.	Starting point. Time.	Route.	In final position by. R'mks.
1.	"B"Batt.Support Coys.only.	Marialinden,	Outpost Line of Resist.—	—	—	Direct.	Z+36mins.
2.	"B"Batt.2 Coys.	Overath.	Main Line of Resist.	Batt.H.Q. Overath	Z+12mins.	Marialinden	Z+1hr.37mins.
	1 Coy.	Hs.Auel.	-do-	Coy.H.Q.	Z	Bridge at F7,1-5,9. Kern.	Z+Mhrs25mins.
	1 Coy.	Steinenbruck	Reserve behind hill C47,W9,8.	Coy.H.Q.	Z	Heiligenhaus - Overath.	Z+3hrs.
3.	"C"Batt.(less detached coy.)2 Coys.	Hoffnungsthal,	Honrath,	Bridge over R.SULZE VOLBERG.	Z	Level Crossing W3,2-7,5.Klein-Eigen-Linden	Z+2hrs.
	1 Coy.	Lughausen.	-do-	Coy.H.Q.	Z	Stocken-Linden.	Z+2hrs.
4.	"C"Batt. Detached Coy.only.	Hohkeppel	Main Line of Resist.	Coy.H.Q.	Z	Unterheide-Vilkerath Bridge S1,1-2,5.Alemich.	Z+2hrs.
5.	"B"Baty.190 Bde.Adv.Bat.	Overath.	Marialinden	Overath Ch.	Z	Bridge W8,8-9,8.	Z+1hr. Will not move.
6.	228th.Field.Coy.R.E.	Bleifold	Outpost Line of Resist.	Fork Rd. W4,8-8,0	Z	Heiligenhaus-Overath.	Z+3hr.37mins.
7.	"B"Coy.M.G.C 1stSect.	Bleifeld	Main Line of Resist.	-do-	Z	-do-	Z+3hrs.5mins.
	1 Sect.	Bleifeld	-do-	-do-	Z	Honrath,Bridge W7,1-5,9 Kern.	Z+3hrs.
8.	A, C & D Batts.190 Bde. R.F.A.	Deutz.	Battle Positions.	Under orders of C/C 190 Bde.R.F.A.	Z	Bensberg-Unter Eschbach.	Z+6hrs.
9.	1st(London) Bde.H.Q.	Rosrath.	Overath.	Bde.H.Q.	Z	Honrath.	Z+3hrs.45mins.

MARCH TABLE C. "Occupy MUCH-DRABENDERHOHE Line."

Serial No.	Unit.	From.	To.	Starting Point Position.	Time.	Route.	In final position by.	Rmks.
1.	"B"Batt.R.Outpost Coy.Posts No.1-4. inclusive.		Much-Drabenderhohe Line.	—	—	Direct.	Z 4hrs.	
	Supporting Coys.only.Marialinden No.3 Post Heck.B.		Marialinden Ch.			Federath.	Z 2hrs.	
2.	"B"Batt.2 Coys.	Overath.	Federath.	Battn.H.Q.	Z 12mins.Marialinden.		Z 1hr.47mins.	
	1 Coy.	Hs.Auel,	-do-	Coy.H.Q.	Z	Kern-Marialinden.	Z 3hrs.20mins.	
	1 Coy.	Steimenbruck	-do-	Coy.H.Q.	Z	Overath-Marialinden.Z 3hrs.30mins.		
3.	"C"Batt.less detached coy. 2 covs.Hoffmungsthal,		Marialinden,	Bridge over R.SULZE,Honrath-Kern, VOLBERG.	Z		Z 4hrs.15mins.	
			-do-	Coy.H.Q.	Z	Stocken-Honrath.	Z 4hrs.15mins.	
4.	"C"Batt. 1 Coy.	Lughausen	Unter-Vilkerath,	Coy.H.Q.	Z	Direct.	Z 40 mins.	
5.	"B"Batt.190 Bde. R.F.A.	Hohkeppel, Marialinden,	Pos.to cover Much-Overath Church. Drabenderhohe Line.		Z	Marialinden,	Z 3hrs.	
6.	228th.Field Coy.R.E.Honrath,		Marialinden, Much-Keltenbach Line	Bridge at W7,1-5,9,Z Fork Roads, Z W 4,8-3,0		Kern, Overath-Marialinden,Z	Z 2hrs.12mins. 7hrs.	
7.	"B"Coy.M.G.C.1½Sect.Bliefeld,				Z	-do-	Z 3hrs.30mins.	
8.	A.C.& D Batts. 2½Sect.Bliefeld,	Deutz,	Federath Marialinden,	-do- Under orders of, O/C 190 Bde.R.F.A.	Z Z	Bensberg-Overath,	Z 7hrs.	
	190 Bde.R.F.A.							
9.	1st.(London)Inf.Bde.Rosrath, H.Q.		Federath,	Bde.H.Q.	Z.	Honrath-Overath-Marialinden	Z 6hrs.20mins.	

APPENDIX "B".

Duties of Picquets on Roads and Railways.

1. Every road and railway crossing the British Zone to the Neutral Zone and unoccupied part of Germany, must be picqueted, the picquet or sentry group being known as control picquet.

The controls will be posted at the point where the road etc crosses the perimeter of the Bridgehead, COLOGNE.

The intervening country between the roads etc., must be patrolled so as to prohibit elicit traffic via trails etc.

2. GENERAL.

(a) Every civilian who wishes to pass through the Line of Control must be in possession of a pass and an identity card. Identity cards need not have photographs of the owner attached until 31st January 1919.

SPECIAL.

(b) The following passes must have the special stamp as set out below. Specimen passes should be issued to all control posts for reference.

PRINTED.	ISSUED BY.	NATURE OF STAMP.	COLOUR OF PASS.	VIDE.
(a)1. Permission to circulate between British occupied area and Belgian or American occupied zone.	Area Com.	Square.	Brown(Male) Green(Female)	M.G.213 para 2a
2. Permission to circulate between British occupied area and Belgian or American occupied area for workmen.	Area or Sub-Area Comdt.	Square or round.	Blue.	M.G.213 para 3a
(b)1. Permission to leave the occupied area to going to unoccupied territory and NOT return.	Sub-Area Comdt.	Square.	Brown(Male) Green(Female)	M.G.213 para 3a
2. Permission to leave the occupied territory to going to unoccupied territory and to return.	Area Comd.	Square.	Brown(Male) Green(Female) & endorsed by Permit office.	M.G.213 para 3b.
3. Permission to go from occupied area to unoccupied area and to Neutral Zone to work	Sub-Area and Area Comdt.	Square.	Blue.	M.G.213 para 3c
(c) Permission to go from British Occupied territory to Allied or Neutral countries.	Area Comd.	Square.	Brown(Male) Green(Female) & endorsed by permit office.	M.G.213 para 4.
(d) Permission to go from unoccupied territory to go into British Occupied Territory.	British Permit Office.	Stamped by D.P.M. 2nd Army.	Telegram & pass issued by Permit Office.	M.G.213 para 5.
(e)1. Permission to go from the Neutral Zone into British Occupied territory to work.	Area or Sub-Area Comdt.	Square.	Blue.	M.G.213 para 6
2. Permission to go from the Neutral Zone into British Occupied Area.	Area or Sub-Area Comdt.	Square.	Brown(Male) Green(Female)	M.G.213 para 6
(f) Permission to go from Neutral or Allied countries to British Occupied Territory.	British Permit Office.	Stamped by D.P.M. 2nd Army.	Telegram & Permit Office pass.	M.G.213 para 7.
(g) Permission to enter British Occupied Territory.	British Permit Office.	Stamped by D.P.M. 2nd Army.	Telegram & Permit Office pass	M.G.213 para 8
(h)1. Permission to circulate by night within British Occupied Territory.	Area or Sub-Area Comdts.	Square or round.	White with red band.	M.G.213 para 9
2. Permission to circulate by night within British Occupied Territory to work.	Area or Sub-Area Comdts.	Square or round.	Blue & endorsed.	M.G.213 para 9

(1) 1. Motor or Motor   Sub-Area   Round.   Pink.   M.G.213 para 1
       Bicycles.   Comdts.
    2. Lorries.   Sub-Area   Round,   Pink.   M.G.213 para 1
                         Comdts.

3. ARREST.
    (a) All civilians attempting to pass through the Line of Control from West to East who are not in possession of their Identity Card (less photograph) and a pass, will be arrested and turned over to the Civil Authorities, a duplicate list of the names being sent to the Sub-Area Commandant every 24 hours.
    (b) All civilians attempting to enter our lines from East to West and are not in possession of their Identity cards and a pass, will have their names taken and be sent back.
    (c) The list of names will be forwarded to Corps for circulation to all Area and Sub-Area Commandants.
    (d) Any person found subsequently to have entered the occupied zone will be dealt with by Summary Court Officer.

4. DUTIES OF PICQUETS ON RAILWAYS.
    An examining picquet will be posted at the nearest station to the perimeter within the Bridgehead.
    Freight Train.
    (a) No trains carrying produce or material of any sort will be allowed to pass to the unoccupied area.
    (b) Empty trains will be allowed to pass into the unoccupied area.
    (c) Trains carrying raw material, coal, etc., will be allowed to enter the Bridgehead from the unoccupied area.

5. PASSENGER TRAINS.
    (a) Certain workmen's trains only will be allowed to and from the Bridgehead and the unoccupied area, and details of these will be sent out as soon as possible from this office.
    (b) Each passenger must be in possession of the Identity card and workman's pass, issued by Area or Sub-Area Commandants, stamped by the D.A.P.M. with the square stamp.
    (c) All passengers travelling from East to West to East contravening this order will be turned off the train at the examining station. (see para 6)
    (d) All passengers travelling from East to West who attempt to enter the Bridgehead without the authorisation papers (identity card and pass), will be detained at the examining station and a report made to the Area Commandant.

6. PASSES. The following coloured passes will be issued by the Provost Branch:-
    Circulation Passes   -   Brown (Male)
    Motor car & Lorries   -   Green (Female)
    Workman's   -   Blue.
    Bicycle   -   Yellow.
    Pass for circulation   -   White pass with Red band across
        by Night.   the centre.

7. Reference para 2, sub-sections (d), (f) and (g) above.
    It should be noted that a telegram sent from the British Permit Office admits the applicant into the British Occupied Area and that the pass is subsequently issued to the applicant at COLOGNE.

APPENDIX "C".

Detailed dispositions of Troops in Outpost Line.

Total detail - 2 Companies.

RIGHT COMPANY.

Disposition of Supports and Company H.Q.

Situation. GRUTZENBACH.
Strength. 3 Officers, 2 Platoons, 2 Lewis Guns held in support to Outpost Line (1, 2 and 3 Posts).
The above Officers and Platoons are billeted in NDR GRUTZENBACH, OBR. GRUTZENBACH and FALKENICH.

Dispositions of Posts etc.

No.1 Post. Situation. GRUBE NICOLAUS.
Strength. 1 Officer, 2 N.C.Os., 14 O.Rs., 1 Lewis Gun.
Sentry. Posted on road leading to SCHMELLENBACH (neutral zone).
Post H.Q. Situated on track leading to Coy.H.Q. (GRUTZENBACH) Distance from Post H.Q. to sentry, 250 yards. Distance from Post H.Q. to Coy.H.Q. 1100 yds (track through woods)

No.2 Post. Situation. BREITENSTEIN.
Strength. 1 Officer, 2 N.C.Os. 14 O.Rs. 1 Lewis Gun.
Sentry. Posted on road leading to MUCH and ECKHAUSEN (Neutral Zone).
Post H.Q. Situated in BREITENSTEIN. Distance from Post H.Q. to Sentry 200 yards. Distance from Post H.Q. to Coy. H.Q. (GRUTZENBACH) 900 yds across country.

No.3 Post. Situation. HENTGES..AF.
Strength. 2 N.C...., 14 O.R. and 1 Lewis Gun.
Sentry. Posted on road leading to GERLINGHAUSEN (neutral zone)
Post H.Q. Situated in HENTGESHAF. Distance from Post H.Q. to sentry, 100 yards. Distance from Post H.Q. to Coy. H.Q. (GRUTZENBACH) 2000 yards across country.

LEFT COMPANY.

Frontage. FEDERATH - KALTENBACH.
Map. Reference. Sheet 2910 OVERATH, and 2911 ENGELSKIRCHEN. The position is held by a series of Posts numbering 4,5,6,7 and 8 with Company H.Q. at DRABENDERHOHE as shown on sketch map attached.
Post No. 4. Lewis Gun Position - good field of fire in southerly direction. Rifle Post firing in southerly direction with a good field of fire. Observation good. Communication between Posts by relay of runners.
Post No.5. Lewis Gun Position - good field of fire covering road leading to EGINGHAUSEN. Observation good.
Post No.6. Lewis Gun and Rifle Section position with two forward positions, numbered on map 1, 2 and 3.
Position 1. Field of fire in direction indicated about 600 yds.
Position 2. Rifle Post covering Road to DRABENDERHOHE and dead ground in front of No. 1 Position.
Position 3. Advanced Observation Post.
Post No.7. Lewis Gun Position - Field of fire is very good but does not cover the approach from MUCH owing to a belt of trees running along the eastern side of the DRABENDERHOHE - MUCH Road. Field of Fire of Rifle Post is good having a range of about 300 yards.
Post No.8. Lewis Gun Position on 300 - contour on the eastern side of road. From this Position it has command of the high ground running from ENGELSKIRCHEN-FORST and also commands a greated part of the main road DRABENDERHOHE - ENGELSKIRCHEN.

APPENDIX "D".

Signal Communications.

Part I. "Occupation.

1. Telephone and Telegraph.
    (a) Forward of Brigade Headquarters. All Units comprising the Brigade Group (less 228th Field Company, R.E.) are in telephone communication with Brigade H.Q. through the existing permanent civil lines.
    (b) From Divisional Headquarters. Existing permanent civil lines connect Divisional H.Q. with Infantry and Artillery Brigade H.Qs.

2. Wireless. The Divisional directing Station is erected at MARIENBURG, and works directly to the three Infantry Brigades.

Part II. "Under Battle Conditions.

The following will be the procedure on receipt of orders :-
(a) Move to Positions of readiness.
(b) Man Battle Positions.
(c) Occupy MUCH - DRABENDERHOHE Line.

1. In the Event of (a)
    (1) Lines. An Advanced Divisional Exchange and Signal Office will be opened at IMMEKEPPEL and a line put through to the Divisional Exchange at MARIENBURG.
    Two lines will be put through from the Advanced Divisional Exchange by means of Field Cable and existing permanent lines to each Infantry Brigade Battle Headquarters, one being for the use of the Artillery Brigade and one for the use of the Infantry Brigade in each case.

    (2) Visual. A Divisional Visual Station will be opened at KAULE ($\frac{3}{4}$ Mile N. of IMMEKEPPEL). This Station can work to the Centre Infantry Brigade at HUFENSUHL and to the Left Infantry Brigade at SCHMITZHOHE direct.

    (3) Wireless. The Divisional Directing Station will be moved up to IMMEKEPPEL. A Trench Set being left at the Rear Divisional Headquarters at MARIENBURG.
    Communication to the three Infantry Brigades will be direct from IMMEKEPPEL.

2. In the event of (b) and (c) as for (a) except that :-
    (1) The Divisional Battle Headquarters Exchange and Signal Office will become the Main Signal Office for the Division and a subsidiary Office only will be left at MARIENBURG.

Army Form C. 2118.

WAR DIARY
or
INTELLIGENCE SUMMARY.
(Erase heading not required.)

Instructions regarding War Diaries and Intelligence Summaries are contained in F. S. Regs., Part II. and the Staff Manual respectively. Title pages will be prepared in manuscript.

Place	Date	Hour	Summary of Events and Information	Remarks and references to Appendices
VOLBERG	1/5/19		Orders received for the following Officers to proceed to the 2/4th Oxfords R.Bucks L.I. 2/Lt G.W. SLEATH M.C. 2/Lt A.C. BELLAMY, 2/Lt J.C. WALLER 2/Lt G.F.V. MEAGRE, 2/Lt C.A. WATTS. The following are posted to the 2/4th. Royal Berks his Regt. T/Lieut a/Capt W.B.V. HUGHES, Lieut H.B. JONES, Lieut P.M. YONGE, 2/Lt J.C. CARVER 2/Lt A.R. WILKINS, E.J. STURMAN J.P. STANLEY and H.E.S. SPURDEN.	
do	2/5/19		The C.O. takes the Battalion on a Route march during the return journey the Battalion does a tactical scheme. The above mentioned Officers proceeded to join their new unit.	
do	3/5/19		Base Orderly Room Sergt. joins us, record Office is now established with the Battalion. The Sergt. of the Batt Played H.Q. Coy at football. Sergt. won. Divine Serv. 3.0. Church Parade held.	

Army Form C. 2118.

WAR DIARY
or
INTELLIGENCE SUMMARY.
(Erase heading not required.)

Instructions regarding War Diaries and Intelligence Summaries are contained in F. S. Regs., Part II. and the Staff Manual respectively. Title pages will be prepared in manuscript.

Place	Date	Hour	Summary of Events and Information	Remarks and references to Appendices
COLBERG	5/5/19		Capt G.E. Deacon arrives from the "Queens" & takes on command of H Coy. We send a draft to Divisional Signals & Artillery of 50 O.R's. Training carried on as usual.	
do	6/5/19		News of probable relief is received, no report to go to Col. N RFLK	
do	7/5/19		The Adjutant Capt E.J.B.M.Jobb M.C proceeds on leave, Lieut C.W. Stratten assumes temporary duties of Adjutant during his absence. The C.O. inspects all men employed on B'du H.Q & is very satisfied with them. A postcard match is played between H.Q & Coy & Divl. Sig. Coy. H.Q win by 3-2.	

WAR DIARY
OR
INTELLIGENCE SUMMARY.

(Erase heading not required.)

Army Form C. 2118.

Place	Date	Hour	Summary of Events and Information	Remarks and references to Appendices
Volseng	8/5/19		Training & Education proceeds as usual. Sitting daily for the Army certification education. In the afternoon the Off's played the Serg's at cricket, this is the first match of the season & results are Off's 81 Serg's 73 winning. The A.D.M.S. inspects the sanitary arrangements & expresses his satisfaction	
do	9/5/19		Training & Education carried as far as feasible most of the Battalion went for a trip down the Rhine	
do	10/5/19		Training & Education proceeds. Cross country run for the Battalion in the afternoon. H.Q. Coy gain a splendid covert's in the evening.	
do	11/5/19		No Church parade owing Padre not available.	
do	12/3/19		Lectim given by Mr Petterns on Arctic Snows. A. Coy gave a concert in the evening, also Serg's a "Smoker". All Officers non involved withs	

WAR DIARY
or
INTELLIGENCE SUMMARY.

(Erase heading not required.)

Army Form C. 2118.

Place	Date	Hour	Summary of Events and Information	Remarks and references to Appendices
15-5-19 JULEPA KALK		14.30	Battalion is relieved by 2.6 Royal Fusiliers & moves back to KALK, the eastern suburbs of Cologne, by train.	R 600 100
KALK	15.5.19		Battalion only now arranging mobilist A Coy are two miles from the nearest other Coy. Billets is very scattered	
do	16.5.19		We march to the RHINE later in line to vaulto of the river then MARSHAL FOCH took the salute cleans.	
	17.5.19		Early morning in artillery & Queen of Honour is marched York before the departure, Basu & 100 um Capt MW Taylor is in command. out in the parade.	

Army Form C. 2118.

WAR DIARY
or
INTELLIGENCE SUMMARY.
(Erase heading not required.)

Place	Date	Hour	Summary of Events and Information	Remarks and references to Appendices
KALK	18.5.19		Church Parade as usual.	
do	19.5.19		We take over all area guards in the district. Preparations are being made to form a Battalion Officers Mess. H Coy men who RALIC from the suburbs, who they have seen under canvas.	00152 00103
do	20.5.19		Other battalion is now doing area Guards. Other Guards carry on with their training daily.	
do	21.5.19		Battalion still furnishing guards. Battalion Officers Mess commenced at dinner.	
do	22.5.19		Guards - duties still being furnished by the unit.	
do	23.5.19		Nothing of special interest to report	
do	24.5.19		C.O. + Adj. went returned from Beirut. Draft on guards received by 5 I.S. Northumberland Fusiliers.	

WAR DIARY
or
INTELLIGENCE SUMMARY.
(Erase heading not required)

Army Form C. 2118.

Place	Date	Hour	Summary of Events and Information	Remarks and references to Appendices
KALK	25.5.19		Guards and duties being found, there are very few men for training. All available are on Education.	
do	26-5-19		Same as yesterday — nothing special to report	
do	27-5-19		Saks Brigade relief of Guards and Picquets. We relieve the 1st Middlesex Regt on the HOHENZOLLERN, NEUE and SUD BRIDGES. Intimation is received at 14.30 hours that civil disturbances are expected in COLOGNE and are in progress in other areas. Bridges are reinforced with men and Lewis Guns. At 21.00 hours all is quiet.	
do	28/5/19		Guards and duties as usual. Officers play the Sergeants of the Battalion at Lawn Tennis, The tournament results in a win for the Officers.	
do	29-5-19		Intimation is received that the Corps Commander will inspect the Brigade on Monday the 2nd June.	
do	30-5-19		Guards and Picquets. Battalion rehearsal for inspection	
do	31-5-19		Brigade rehearsal for inspection	

Ewen Cameron Lieut. Col.
9th East Surrey Regt.

WAR DIARY 9th East Surrey Regt

Army Form C. 2118.

WAR DIARY
or
INTELLIGENCE SUMMARY.

45B
5 sheets

Place	Date	Hour	Summary of Events and Information	Remarks and references to Appendices
KALK	1/6/19		Church Parade at YMCA Cinema.	
do	2/6/19		Corps Commanders inspection of the 1st London Brigade. The 9th Bn Middlesex Regt and 9th East Surrey Regt also 1st London Fld Coy light Trench Mortar Battery are drawn up on the EXERZIER PLATZ. Four hrs Transport attends. After the inspection the Battalions march past and return to billets. The Barrack Rooms are inspected. The Corps Commander (Gen Sir Aylmer Haldane K.C.B.) expresses his complete satisfaction. In the evening to celebrate the opening of the Battalion Officers Mess a Concert and Dinner is given. There are representatives of all Branches of the Service present.	
do	3/6/19		To celebrate the Kings Birthday a general holiday is given the Battalion parades at 0900 hours in the MARKET SQUARE in Full order. The Commanding Officer addresses the men, the National Anthem is played by the Band and cheers are given for His Majesty the King.	

WAR DIARY 9th East Surrey Regt

Army Form C. 2118.

INTELLIGENCE SUMMARY.

(Erase heading not required.)

Place	Date	Hour	Summary of Events and Information	Remarks and references to Appendices
KALK	4/6/19		The Guards on the Hohenzollern, NEVE and SUD BRIDGES are changed. The men work well to turn out a Guard Parade. The Brigadier General attends the Duties Parade at 1000 hours.	
do.	5/6/19		A draft of 200 private soldiers arrive from the 23rd Bn. Royal Fusiliers. Training continues.	
do.	6/6/19		All available men are sent to the Gas hut and on the Rifle Range. Draft is inspected by the Commanding Officer.	
do.	7/6/19		Education. Inspection of billets by C.O.	
do.	8/6/19		Church Parade service.	
do.	9/6/19		Whit Monday - a general holiday for all troops	
do	10/6/19		Pool shooting on the Rifle Range at BRUCK.	
do	11/6/19		Changing of Guards on HOHENZOLLERN, NEVE and SUD BRIDGES	
do	12/6/19		Corps Commander inspects the Guards on the Bridges.	

WAR DIARY 9th East Surrey Regt

or

~~INTELLIGENCE SUMMARY~~

(Erase heading not required.)

Army Form C. 2118.

Instructions regarding War Diaries and Intelligence Summaries are contained in F. S. Regs., Part II and the Staff Manual respectively. Title pages will be prepared in manuscript.

Place	Date	Hour	Summary of Events and Information	Remarks and references to Appendices
KALK	13/6/19		Guards and Training, Gas hut at KEULE	
do	14/6/19		Commanding Officer inspects billets. Education.	
do	15/6/19		Church Parade.	
do	16/6/19		Training and Education	
do	17/6/19		Inspection of Battalion by Brigadier General W.M. WITHYCOMBE C.M.G., D.S.O. who has assumed command of the 1st London Brigade.	
do	18/6/19		Changing of Garrison Guards.	
do	19/6/19		Intimation is received that preparations are to be made for an immediate advance into German territory on "T" day. "T" day is expected to be the 20th inst. All surplus Kit is dumped and arrangements made to move.	
do	20/6/19		"T" is postponed until further orders. All troops are in readiness to move.	
do	21/6/19		Training on Rifle Range and Education	
do	22/6/19		Church Parade.	

WAR DIARY 9th East Surrey Regt   Army Form C. 2118.

or

INTELLIGENCE SUMMARY.

(Erase heading not required.)

Place	Date	Hour	Summary of Events and Information	Remarks and references to Appendices
KALK	23/6/19		Training. Information is received that the enemy is likely to attempt the destruction of the HOHENZOLLERN, NEUE and SUD BRIDGES tonight. All precautions are taken and extra sentries placed near the Bridges. All is quiet.	
do	24/6/19		News that Peace has been signed is received.	
do	25/6/19		Changing of Garrison Guards. The Divisional Commander attends the Guard Mounting Parade.	
do	26/6/19		Education. Rifle Range at BRUCK - pool shooting is carried on.	
do	27/6/19		Coys await the disposal of Company Commanders for education and general training.	
do	28/6/19		Commanding Officer inspects billets	
do	29/6/19		Church Parade.	
do	30/6/19		Education and training. Pool shooting on rifle range.	

Swanson Lt Col
Comdg 9th East Surrey Regt

NOMINAL ROLL OF OFFICERS.

Rank.	Name.		Remarks.
Lt-Col.	E.A.CAMERON,	CMG.DSO.	Commanding Officer.
Major.	J.C.BROWN,	MC.	Second-in-Command.
"	G.O.SEARLE.		Div.Educational Off.
"	W.G.WEST.		Leave.
Capt.	M.W.TAYLOR,	MC.	
"	G.E.DEACON.		
"	L.I.DEACON.		
"	F.C.READ.		R.A.S.C.
"	E.H.B.NOBBS,	MC.	Adjutant.
"	F.J.GAYWOOD,	MC.	A.D.R.T.
"	H.L.JONES,	MC.	Staff Capt.Civil Dts.
"	G.L.LAWLOR.		R.A.M.C.
Lieuts.	C.W.HAWTIN.		Asst. Adjutant.
"	B.H.STANTON.		
"	H.J.LANCASTER,	MC.	
"	G.L.WHITE,	MC.	Sports Officer.
"	E.COLEBROOK,	MC.	
"	R.K.FAULKNER.		Course.
"	H.V.KERCKHOVE,	MC.	Hospital.
"	C.E.TEVERSHAM.		Leave.
"	H.R.TUCKER.		Leave.
"	E.J.WOOD,	MC.	Leave.
"	C.S.IRONS,	MC.	Signal Officer.
"	A.W.ENGLAND.		
"	C.STUART.		Leave.
"	S.E.BENNETT.		Divisional Baths.
"	WEST.		Posted for records.
" & Q.M.	E.ABRAMS.		Quarter-Master.
2/Lts.	G.R.GARRAWAY.		Transport Officer.
"	H.W.GREGORY.		Lewis Gun Officer.
"	R.JACOBS.		
"	P.J.POPE.		Course, England.
"	A.STEPHENS.		Educational Officer.
"	G.L.WILLIAMS,	MC.	
"	E.NELSON.		Hospital.
"	C.W.CRAFTER.		R.A.O.D.
"	E.W.CREEGAN.		Course, England.
"	R.F.HOWSHIP,	MC,	2nd London Bde.
"	G.SIMKINS.		
"	C.L.SMITH.		
"	J.S.HASTIE.		
"	E.W.DOVE-MEDOWS.		
"	MATTHEWS.		2nd Army H.Q.
"	A.H.WHITE.		

Ewen Cameron

Lieut.-Col.,
Comdg. 8th.Bn. EAST SURREY REGT.

26.6.1919.

NOMINAL ROLL OF OFFICERS.

Rank.	Name.		Remarks.
T/Lt.Col.	E.A.Cameron,	CMG, DSO.	Commanding Officer.
T/Major.	J.C.Brown,	MC	Second in Command.
"	G.O.Searle.		Divisional Education Officer.
"	W.G.West.		
T/Capt.	M.W.Taylor,	MC	
"	G.E.Deacon.		
"	L.I.Deacon.		
"	F.C.Read.		R.A.S.C.
"	G.L.Lawlor.		R.A.M.C.
T/Lt. A/Capt.	E.H.B.Nobbs.	MC.	Adjutant.
Lt.TF. A/Capt.	H.L.Jones,	MC.	Staff Capt. Civil Duties.
T/Lieut.	C.W.Hawtin.		Asst. Adjt. On Leave.
"	B.M.Stanton.		
"	H.J.Lancaster,	MC.	
"	G.L.White,	MC.	
"	E.Colebrook,	MC.	
" S.R.	H.V.Kerckhove,	MC.	
"	C.E.Teversham.		
" S.R.	H.R.Tucker.		Education Officer.
"	E.J.Wood,	MC.	
"	C.S.Irons,	MC.	Signal Officer.
"	A.W.England.		
"	C.Stuart.		
"	West.		Scots Rifles.
" S.R.	H.N.Bailey.		
Lt. & Q.M.	E.Abrams.		Quartermaster. (General list).
T/2/Lieuts.	G.R.Garraway.		Transport Officer.
"	H.W.Gregory.		Leave.
"	R.Jacobs.		Sports Officer.
"	P.J.Pope.		Course, England.
"	A.Stephens.		R.A.O.C.
"	E.Nelson.		Leave.
"	E.W.Creegan.		
"	R.F.Howship,	MC.	
"	G.Simkins.		Hospital.
"	C.L.Smith.		
"	J.S.Hastie.		
" S.R.	E.W.Dove-Medows.		Hospital.
"	Matthews.		2nd Army H.Q.
"	A.H.White.		

EHBNobbs
Capt & Adjt

Lieut. Colonel. Commanding.
9th. Bn. EAST SURREY REGIMENT.

30.7.19.

To: H.Q., 1st London Brigade.

Herewith War Diary for the month of July, please.

Ewen A Cameron

Lieut. Colonel. Commanding.
9th. Bn. EAST SURREY REGIMENT.

9th BATTALION,
EAST SURREY
REGIMENT.
No. ES 361
Date 1.8.19.

WAR DIARY 9th East Surrey Regt.
or INTELLIGENCE SUMMARY.

Army Form C. 2118.

46B
6 sheets

Place	Date	Hour	Summary of Events and Information	Remarks and references to Appendices
KOLN KALK	1/7/19		The Commanding Officer inspects the Battalion. In the afternoon hears OBERHOLM of the USA Army instruct Companies in Baseball. Bayonet fighting & Boxing is also carried out under Company instructors.	
	2/7/19		Cleaning of Garrison Quarters.	
	3/7/19		General Holiday granted to commemorate Peace. 200 (All ranks) proceed for a trip down the Rhine commencing at 08.30 hours terminating at 19.00 hours.	
	4/7/19		CO inspects Billets. Training & execution.	
	5/7/19		Church Parade	
	6/7/19			
	7/7/19		Coys proceed to the Gas test KEULE when men are run through the gas test.	
	8/7/19		Education & musketry training. Preparation are being made for Annual musketry classification which is to be fired at Chorhorst.	

WAR DIARY
or
INTELLIGENCE SUMMARY

9th Bn East Surrey Regt
Army Form C. 2118.

Place	Date	Hour	Summary of Events and Information	Remarks and references to Appendices
KALK	9/7/19 10/7/19 11/7/19		Changing Garrison Guards. Firing of the Elementary Musketry Course at Brück Elementary Musketry Course continued.	
"	12/7/19		Battalion Route march in full marching order, after which majority of Batt. proceeded to Cologne Races.	
"	13/7/19		Church Parade.	
"	14/7/19		Musketry training in barracks, preparatory to the General Musketry Course.	
"	15/7/19		Battalion is relieved by the 11th Queens in Kalk area & 00.'07 relieves 11th Queens in the left sub-sector of Divisional advances front. We are now under canvas at EHRENHOVEN.	
EHRESHOVEN	16/7/19		Rifle Range for Musketry course and arrange camp.	
do	17/7/19		A and D Coys arrivals to fire G.M.C. & Coy training for Coy for Coy in training complete.	

Army Form C. 2118.

9th Bn. East Surrey Regt.

WAR DIARY
or
INTELLIGENCE SUMMARY.
(Erase heading not required.)

Instructions regarding War Diaries and Intelligence Summaries are contained in F. S. Regs., Part II. and the Staff Manual respectively. Title pages will be prepared in manuscript.

Place	Date	Hour	Summary of Events and Information	Remarks and references to Appendices
EHRESHOVEN	18/7/19		Musketry and Coy training. Education. Practical training in afternoon	
do	19/7		General holiday to celebrate Peace. The Sergeants play the Officers at Cricket.	
do	20/7		Church Parade	
do	21/7		Musketry. Education and Company training. The wet weather has set in again and firing on the range is most unpleasant.	
do	22/7		Firing this morning was impossible owing to heavy down pour. Training and education in dining room continues.	
do	23/7		Musketry and training. The Band and Drums are practising for VI Corps Tattoo tonight later.	
do	24/7		Weather is still very bad. Firing. Education and company training.	
do	25/7		Nothing of interest to report. Training continues.	
do	26/7		ditto	
do	27/7		Church Parade	

9th Bn East Surrey Regt. Army Form C. 2118.

WAR DIARY
or
INTELLIGENCE SUMMARY
(Erase heading not required.)

Place	Date	Hour	Summary of Events and Information	Remarks and references to Appendices
EHRESHOVEN	28/7		"B" Company under the Command of Captain L.T. DEACON won the Brigade Inter Company turn out competition.	
do	29/7		Musketry and Education	
do	30/7		"A" and "D" companies fired firing G.M.C.	
do	31/7		Brigade Horse Show. We won six of the twelve events, and came second in two other events.	

Swanserman Lieut Col.
Comdg 9th East Surrey Regt.

WAR DIARY
INTELLIGENCE SUMMARY

Army Form C. 2118.

9th East Surrey Regt.

47.B
7shels

Place	Date	Hour	Summary of Events and Information	Remarks and references to Appendices
EHRESHOVEN	1/8		Musketry, Company and Educational training.	
"	2/8		Training and final preparations for Battalion Sports. We win the Brigade inter Battalion Tug O War competition.	
"	3/8		Sunday. A most successful Sports meeting was held to-day only marred by the inclement weather. Great enthusiasm was shown by all ranks to make the days success. Many visitors were present including Major General Sir R S LAWFORD K.C.B. (Commanding London Division) Brig. General W M WITHYCOMBE CMG DSO (Commanding 1st London Infantry (Bde.)) Members of the Divisional and Brigade Staff. Representatives from the NAVY, & MAAC CHURCH ARMY etc. The Band played selections during the afternoon. Results. Inter Coy Relay Race won by L/Cpl Groves B. Coy. High Jump " Lieut A H White A Coy Long Jump " Lieut H R Kerckhove B " Putting the weight " Sgt GREENSLADE B " Tug-of-War Competition A and B. (tied)	

No. ES.789
date 2.9.19

WAR DIARY
or
INTELLIGENCE SUMMARY.
(Erase heading not required.)

Army Form C. 2118.

Place	Date	Hour	Summary of Events and Information	Remarks and references to Appendices
EHRESHOVEN	cont		Results 100yds Flat Race won by Lieut H.R. KERCKHOVE	B.Coy
			Sack Race " " " Pte HIRST	A Coy
			120 yards Hurdles (Open) " " " J.1. Wulgoose	Brigade Schoolmaster
			Three Legged Race " " " Sgt Honeychurch + Millman	B. Coy
			440 yards – (Open) " " " Sgt. CLARK	4th Middlx. Regt.
			Inter Coy Tug of War won " " "	B. Coy
			Drill Contest – Mindfold " " "	C "
			220 yards Flat Race " " " Lieut H.R. KERCKHOVE	B. Coy
			Three Mile Flat – (Open) " " " Pte BLANDFORD	T.M.B. (9th E.S.R)
			440 yds Flat " " " Pte JAMES	D. Coy
			Pillow fight " " " Sgt GREENSLADE	B "
			120 yds Hurdle Race " " " Lieut A.H. WHITE	A "
			100yds Flat (Officers) " " " Lieut STUART	C "
			Obstacle Race " " " Corpl. Stanley	C "
			Mule Race " " " Pte Gowring	A "

Army Form C. 2118.

WAR DIARY
or
INTELLIGENCE SUMMARY.
(Erase heading not required.)

Place	Date	Hour	Summary of Events and Information	Remarks and references to Appendices
EHRESHOVEN			Results cont.	
			One (1) Mile Flat Race. won by Pte Havelock A Coy	
			Veterans Race 100 yds " " C.S.M. Howell B "	
			Tug of War — (Open) " " Qd East Surrey Regt.	
			120 yds Hurdle Race (open) " " Pte Neal Coy 9th E.S.R.	
			220 yds Flat — (all Officers) " " Lieut Col. B.A. Cannon O.M.C.N.S.O	
"	4-8-19		General Holiday. majority of the Batt attended Divisional tattoo at twilight provision.	
"	5.8.19		Musketry Training, firing General Musketry course at Kemp Christloor. C.O. awarded 1st Prize in Div Wars Slow 1/- for Officers Classes the Batt carried four prizes out of a possible nine	
"	6.8.19		Batt Rifle meeting commenced. General musketry course suspended temporarily until Bou Rifle meeting finished.	
"	7.8.19		Training, education & general parades.	

WAR DIARY
or
INTELLIGENCE SUMMARY

Army Form C. 2118.

Place	Date	Hour	Summary of Events and Information	Remarks and references to Appendices
Ehrenfeld	8.6.19		Recreation & General Training carried on. During the afternoon recreational training - Usual training Programme	
do	9.6.19		Church Parade.	
do	10.6.19		C Coy proceeded to the EXERZIERPLATZ, near Cologne to compete against representatives of the Brigade of the Division in a "Inter Coy competition". They obtained second Place. In the winning the Heats of Bde Sports	
do	11.6.19		was run off.	
do	12.6.19.		Training in the morning : from 14.00 hours Bde Sports A very successful afternoon. This Battalion obtained Second Place in points, the 7th Middx Regt obtain- ing first Place.	
do	13.8.19.		Half Battalion Parade remained training, for Rem. sent a refrigerator team into the Usual training.	
do	14.7.19		Cologne Aquatic Sports. B Coy had a dinner & were in their honor for obtaining most points in Battn Sports, afterwards a concert was held.	

Army Form C. 2118.

WAR DIARY
or
INTELLIGENCE SUMMARY.
(Erase heading not required.)

Instructions regarding War Diaries and Intelligence Summaries are contained in F. S. Regs., Part II. and the Staff Manual respectively. Title pages will be prepared in manuscript.

Place	Date	Hour	Summary of Events and Information	Remarks and references to Appendices
Chiseldon	15/5/19		Training as usual.	
do	16/5/19		Training & inspection of camp by the Commanding Officer	remainder
do	17/5/19		Church Parade.	
do	18/5/19		B Coy continue firing. General musketry Course.	
do	19/5/19		D Battalion - General training	
			B Coy final C. M. C. - usual training - The C.O. was last known to be in the Army store shows for Infantry losses last known to be "in" duty.	
do	20/5/19		Divisional Commander inspected the Bath at 09.15 hours today, afterwards inspecting Coys carried on training. The comf. & C Coy firing on the range.	
do	21/5/19		C Coy continue firing - Corps Commander visits the Battalion - inspecting Range Comp - Conf at work	
do	22/5/19		Firing on range - General training.	
do	23/5/19		C.O. inspects camp.	
do	24/5/19		Church Parade - Casuals firing training carried out firm from 07.30 hours until 19.00 hours	

WAR DIARY or INTELLIGENCE SUMMARY.

Army Form C. 2118.

Instructions regarding War Diaries and Intelligence Summaries are contained in F. S. Regs., Part II. and the Staff Manual respectively. Title pages will be prepared in manuscript.

(Erase heading not required.)

Place	Date	Hour	Summary of Events and Information	Remarks and references to Appendices
Churlow	25/8/19		Completion of General Musketry Course. Bn Cross Country Run – commenced at 15. 30 hours. 9th East Surrey's first. 7. Middx Regt second. 23 – third.	
"	26/8/19		Commenced of Renewed Rifle Meeting – weather very inclement. Educational training during morning – percentional training in afternoon.	
"	27/8/19		General training – Battalion dancing class for all ranks commenced – great interest being shown.	
"	28/8/19		Education in morning, afternoon – afternoon – Officers had a "Each training" dinner & dancing	
"	29/8/19		Football match versus 23rd Middx result G.E.S.R. 3 – 23 Middx winning 4. Bn rifle meeting commenced. 2 firsts + 3 thirds in having obtained	

Army Form C. 2118.

WAR DIARY
or
INTELLIGENCE SUMMARY.
(Erase heading not required.)

Instructions regarding War Diaries and Intelligence Summaries are contained in F. S. Regs., Part II. and the Staff Manual respectively. Title pages will be prepared in manuscript.

Place	Date	Hour	Summary of Events and Information	Remarks and references to Appendices
Chisledon	30/6/19		The Commanding Officer inspected the Camp. Our tug of war team pulled against the R.A.C. & won, we are now in the semi-final to be II Corps Championship - slip having beaten the 1/7th Middlesex Regt and 23rd Royal Fusiliers.	
do	31/6/19		Church Parade.	

WAR DIARY or INTELLIGENCE SUMMARY

Army Form C. 2118.
9th East Surrey Regt

Place	Date	Hour	Summary of Events and Information	Remarks and references to Appendices
Chocques	1/9/19		Battalion relieves 23rd Middlesex Regt in Right Sub Section of Divisional Front	O.O. 105.
Eugleborch	2/9/19		A.B. & D Coys at Eugleborch. carry on with Training	
"	3/9/19		A.B. & D Coys at Eugleborch. carry on with Training. Battalion during the morning the Forts Pass were found to us by Artillery Instructors of outpost time.	
"	4/9/19		Divisional Cross Country Run took place commencing at Govrath — our team secured second place — Lt Bell obtained 1st — 2nd — 4th — 5th. General Training — In the evening in Major the 23rd Middlesex afterwards winning by 2 goals to nil.	
"	5/9/19			
"	6/9/19		C.O. inspected camp of Eugleberche — Orders received relieve 23rd Middlesex & as commanded as 19 c Roues huilt. First innings 23rd Midd 30 9th East Surreys 109 Second innings 39 9th East Surreys at 17. 20 Runs won by own wickets 107	

9th BATTALION,
EAST SURREY
REGIMENT.

No. ____
Date 7.10.19
E5. 1/90

9th East Surrey Regt
Army Form C. 2118.

WAR DIARY
or
INTELLIGENCE SUMMARY.
(Erase heading not required.)

Instructions regarding War Diaries and Intelligence Summaries are contained in F. S. Regs., Part II. and the Staff Manual respectively. Title pages will be prepared in manuscript.

Place	Date	Hour	Summary of Events and Information	Remarks and references to Appendices
	7/9/19 Eupatoria		Church Parade in Lutheran Church Eugelskirchen	
	8/9/19	do	B + D Companies carry out Bathing. A + C coys for two hours only.	
	9/9/19	do	B, D coys carry out company tactical schemes.	
	10/9/19	do.	Inter Coln. lectures on the British Empire at 10 o'clock today. In the semi-final of the Rugby of the Rugby football pulled the Corps semi-final against the 93rd. R.Q.M. winning in the first two pulls. In the final we were completa against the 35th R.Q.M. + lost.	
	11/9/19		The Inspector of "mens" messing visited + inspected the cooking arrangements. He expressed his satisfaction in the method adopted for the feeding of the men.	
	12/9/19		Lecture for one Route – Company training during the remainder of the morning.	
	13/9/19		Lecture on "America + Great Britain" by the Hon Crawford Vaughan.	

9th East Surrey Regt

Army Form C. 2118.

WAR DIARY
or
INTELLIGENCE SUMMARY.
(Erase heading not required.)

Place	Date	Hour	Summary of Events and Information	Remarks and references to Appendices
Cuypobucher	14.9.19.		Church Parade.	
"	15.9.19.		The G.O.C viewed on platoon of "B" Coy doing a tactical scheme.	
	16.9.19		Review Divisional Horse Show was held at Ourack today - General Furicary for all units of "B" Division - "B" Battalion did very well, the C.O. & "Kitty" winning first in Officers Charges, our pack mule also won first. Sgt Longelin secured second in bending race - Sgt Longelin secured fourth. Cookers, NCO's mess, & Mallen The C.O. on "Kitty" secured second in her class - Y Ride = water Cart: altogether in secured
			2 . 1st.
			2 . 2nd
			1 . 3rd
			3 . 4th
"	17.9.19.		Education & General Training
	18.9.19		Conferences at aufoat of Coy Commanders
	19.9.19		Education & general training
	20.9.19		The C.O inspected the camp at Cuypobucher.

WAR DIARY or INTELLIGENCE SUMMARY

9th East Surrey Regt

Army Form C. 2118.

Place	Date	Hour	Summary of Events and Information	Remarks and references to Appendices
Engelskirchen	21/9/19		Church Parade.	
do	22/9/19		Training carried on in during early morning to heavy rain.	
do	23/9/19		Announcement of Control Posts formed – abbreviating the through demobilization. Outpost line owing to lack of men –	O.O. 109
do	24/9/19		Companies engaged on platoon & coy tactical schemes.	
do	25/9/19		Education & recreational training.	
do	26/9/19		Battalion attended Battn. Sports at Engelskirchen. night training.	
do	27/9/19		C.O. inspects account. A concert is given by Mrs May Jayle's party in the Recreationhüttes – after the concert the party dined with Mrs.	
do	28/9/19		Church Parade cancelled owing to heavy rain	
do	29/9/19		Educational training	
do	30/9/19		Corps Horse Show held at EXERZIER. PLATZ KALK. C.O. copy 1st prize on "KITTY". The makeup of Cap: "KITTY" has won.	

WAR DIARY
INTELLIGENCE SUMMARY

Army Form C. 2118.

49 B
5 sheets

Place	Date	Hour	Summary of Events and Information	Remarks and references to Appendices
Bugulchuchu	1/10/19		Company training – Batt: Cross Country run commenced at 15:30 hours at KINDHAR. Our H.Q. team won by 70 points, our Company team being fourth placed. We ran the challenge Cup now for second consecutive time.	
	2/10/19		Education for two Coys at Bugulchuchu.	
	3/10/19		The camp is being struck today – All numan moving into fields.	
	4/10/19		Battalion continuing the evacuation of camp – all men are in tents now.	
	5/10/19		Church Parade.	
	6/10/19		B & D Coys carried out Coy training – recreation for all Coys in the afternoon.	
	7/10/19		The High Sheriff of London Sir William Smith and his wife Lady Smith visited the Battalion to day Sunday and afterwards toured the camp & workshops etc the others – afterwards	

9th BATTALION
EAST SURREY
REGT.
E.S.2.
31.10.19

WAR DIARY
or
INTELLIGENCE SUMMARY.

Army Form C. 2118.

Place	Date	Hour	Summary of Events and Information	Remarks and references to Appendices
Englefontein	8/10/19		All officers assembled at 14 o'clock for mounted paper chase - Room Major Brown & Lt Stanton - run lasted for an hour - at 15 officers incl Coy Cross country run B Coy won the winners	
"	9/10/19		B, D Coys education - Sergeant Major & Battalion team at football today & won by two goals	
"	10/10/19		Coy training carried out - y ke O.C. Commencing worked Batt & inspected extra	
"	11/10/19		Inspection of gottas Uniforms winning by 1 goal B Coy at football H 4 - B 3.	
"	12/10/19		Church Parade - at 14:00 hours at Officers at 11:0 for a mounted paper chase - stars Capt Deacon & Sgt Wilmot	

Army Form C. 2118.

WAR DIARY
or
INTELLIGENCE SUMMARY.
(Erase heading not required.)

Instructions regarding War Diaries and Intelligence Summaries are contained in F. S. Regs., Part II. and the Staff Manual respectively. Title pages will be prepared in manuscript.

Place	Date	Hour	Summary of Events and Information	Remarks and references to Appendices
			[handwritten entries, largely illegible]	

Army Form C. 2118.

WAR DIARY
or
INTELLIGENCE SUMMARY.
(Erase heading not required.)

Instructions regarding War Diaries and Intelligence Summaries are contained in F. S. Regs., Part II. and the Staff Manual respectively. Title pages will be prepared in manuscript.

Place	Date	Hour	Summary of Events and Information	Remarks and references to Appendices
Engelsfurt	22/10/19		Tactical scheme for officers carried out at MARKT. In the opinion of the [umpires?] for the day, won by winning Regt. Winners - 7th Cavalry Regt. Second - 9th Cavalry Regt. Third - 23rd Cavalry Regt at KINDLAC.	OO...
	23/10/19		D.H.Q. renews 23rd Cavalry [Regt?] headquarters at [...]	
	24/10/19		Battalion [marched?] to STEINBACH	
	25/10/19		C.O. inspected billets at ENGELSFURT	
	26/10/19		Rode to church parade	
	27/10/19		[...]	
	28/10/19		[...]	
	29/10/19		[...]	
	30/10/19		[...]	
	31/10/19		[...]	

John [signature]
LIEUT. COLONEL,
COMDG. 8th BN. EAST SURREY REGT.

NOMINAL ROLL OF OFFICERS.

Rank.	Name.	Remarks.
T/Lt-Col.	E.A.Cameron, CMG, DSO.	Commanding Officer.
Reg.Lt. T/Maj.	J.C.Brown, MC.	Second in Command.
T/Major.	F.C.West.	Officers' Club.
T/Capt.	M.W.Taylor, MC.	Leave to Venice.
"	G.E.Deacon.	
"	L.I.Deacon.	Leave.
"	F.C.Read.	R.A.S.C.
"	Nelson.	R.A.M.C.
T/Lt. A/Capt.	E.H.B.Robbs, MC.	Adjutant. Leave to Venice.
T/Lieut.	C.R.Hastin.	Assistant Adjutant.
"	E.H.Stanton.	
"	R.J.Lancaster, MC.	
"	G.L.White, MC.	
"	E.H.Colebrook, MC.	
" S.R.	R.V.Herokove, MC.	
" S.R.	H.R.Tucker.	Education Officer.
"	C.K.Taversham.	
"	E.J.Wood, MC.	
"	C.B.Irons, MC.	Signal Officer.
"	A.W.England.	Course.
"	West.	Scots Rifles.
" S.R.	H.M.B.Bailey.	
"	P.J.Pope.	
" & QM.	N.Abrams.	Quartermaster. (General List).
T/2/Lts.	G.R.Garraway.	Transport Officer.
"	B.Jacobs.	Sports Officer.
"	R.Stephens.	R.A.D.C.
"	E.Nelson.	
"	R.W.Creegan.	
"	C.L.Smith.	
"	J.D.Hastie.	
"	A.H.White.	
"	Matthews.	2nd Army H...
" S.R.	E.W.Dove-Medows.	Staff Captain Civil Duties.

[signature]

1.10.19.

Lieut.Colonel. Commanding.
9th. Bn. EAST SURREY REGIMENT.

NOMINAL ROLL OF OFFICERS.

Rank.	Name.	Remarks.
Lt.Col.	E.A.Cameron.CMG.DSO.	Commanding Officer.
Major.	J.C.Brown.MC.	2nd.in Command.
Captain.	M.W.Taylor.MC.	
"	E.H.B.Nobbs.MC.	Adjutant.
"	L.I.Deacon.	
"	G.E.Deacon.	
"	G.L.Lawlor.	M.O. (R.A.M.C.)
Lieut.	C.W.Hawtin.	Assistant Adjutant.
"	B.M.Stanton.	
"	H.J.Lancaster.MC.	
"	G.L.White.MC.	
"	E.H.Colebrook.MC.	
"	H.V.Kerckhove.MC.	
"	H.R.Tucker.	Education Officer. (Leave.)
"	C.E.Teversham.	
"	E.J.Wood.MC.	
"	C.S.Irons.MC.	Signal Officer.
"	A.W.England.	
"	West..	Scot. Rifles.
"	H.M.S.Bailey.	
"	P.J.Pope.	Hospital.
"	F.C.Read.	
" & QM.	E.Abrams.	Quartermaster.
2nd.Lt.	G.R.Garroway.	Transport Officer.
"	R.Jacobs.	Sports Officer.
"	E.Nelson.	
"	E.W.Creegan.	Leave.
"	C.L.Smith.	
"	J.S.Hastie.	
"	A.H.White.	
"	E.W.Dove-Medows.